Life's Journey

Personal Journal

Darryl S. Doane
Rose D. Sloat

With special comments and observations by
David S. Doane, Ph.D., Psychologist

HRD Press, Inc. • Amherst • Massachusetts

Published by: HRD Press, Inc.
22 Amherst Road
Amherst, MA 01002
413-253-3488
800-822-2801 (U.S. and Canada)
413-253-3490 (fax)
www.hrdpress.com

ISBN 978-1-59996-254-2

Editorial services by Sally M. Farnham
Production services by Jean Miller
Cover design by Eileen Klockars

Life's Journey

Personal Journal

Eureka!
"I have found it."

Now that you have found or discovered your place to stand, we thought that it was very fitting to return to Archimedes for inspiration to move forward with that discovery. Archimedes was the inspiration for "Find Your Place to Stand!" History tells us that while Archimedes was in his bath, he was the first to use the expression Eureka! (I have found it!) This exclamation came when he discovered that a body displaces its own bulk in water when immersed. He, therefore, exclaimed, "Eureka!" Well, now it's your turn to rejoice.

What will you do with your discovery of self? Here is where your own internal power and gift of free will come into play. You have selected the Life Units that you identified as significant in your own life. You've located your present position and where you would like to be. You have taken into account the specific actions required to build the bridge from your present to your future. The totality of all your selected Life Units equals that future. Where do you go from here? What will you do? Your discovery of having found out so much about yourself is not enough. The time is now upon you to take action and to make your journey.

Please give yourself permission to make a difference with your own life. Only you can do it. Only you can take all that you have discovered and achieve the next level. Consider how far you have already come and all you have allowed yourself to focus on and invest in. How sad it would be to not nourish and grow that discovery of self you have made. You've earned it! You have opened the door to your own future. Now give yourself permission to walk through that door and embrace that which you know is yours.

I am aware of my current status in each area of concentration. I am also aware of where I want to be in my identified future. If I give myself permission to take the appropriate actions based upon this awareness, I will see a significant impact upon my own life as I allow my own actions to propel me toward my own future.

A journey begins with one step at a time and here I may record my daily, weekly, monthly, and yearly progress. This journal is for the documentation of my own progress, questions, concerns, and feelings encountered as I move toward my "right future."

As I completed each Life Unit that I selected, I plotted my identified Place to Stand (where I am at now) for that Life Unit. I then was to plot my desired future for that Life Unit.

So here are the next steps for you to take to attain the Right Future.

1. Transfer each Life Unit to your Wheel of Focus.

2. Graph out your Place to Stand for selected Life Units on the Wheel of Focus.

3. Graph out your Desired Future for selected Life Units on the Wheel of Focus.

4. Identify the gaps that exist (if any) between where you are currently at and your determined future.

5. Identify *specific actions* to build your performance bridge from where you are currently at to your own future (where you want to be).

6. Transfer each Wheel of Focus to your Life Pattern.

7. Give yourself permission to take action and create your own future.

8. Use your *Life's Journey Personal Journal* to track and document your progress.

Recommended Procedure to Attain
the Right Future

1. **Transfer each Life Unit to your Wheel of Focus.** The Wheel of Focus
    brings together all of your personally selected Life Units for a particular Life
    Focus Area. It is a wonderful visualization for use in achieving clarity of
    understanding of where you are right now in your life and where you want
    and need to be.

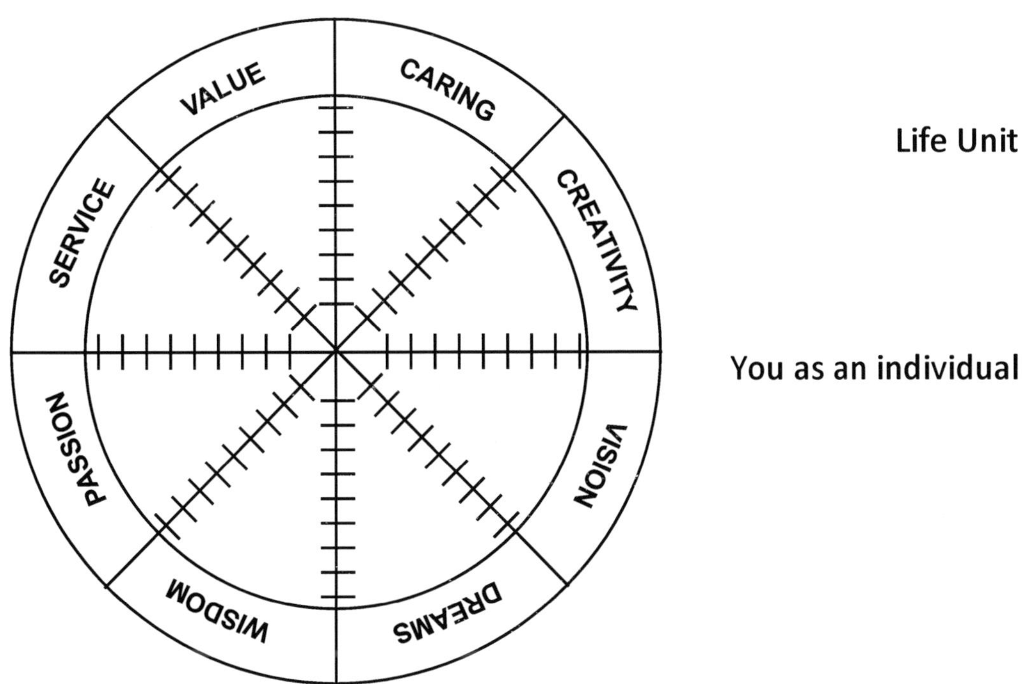

Life Unit

You as an individual

2. **Graph out your Place to Stand for selected Life Units on the Wheel of Focus.** By connecting (graphic out) your identified Place to Stand for each Life Unit, you have brought into full view your foundation upon which you shall build your chosen future. This represents where you are at right now. Love it or hate it, embrace it or despise it, you have brought to the surface a critical awareness of self that once accepted gives you the ability to change, control, direct, and build upon if you so choose!

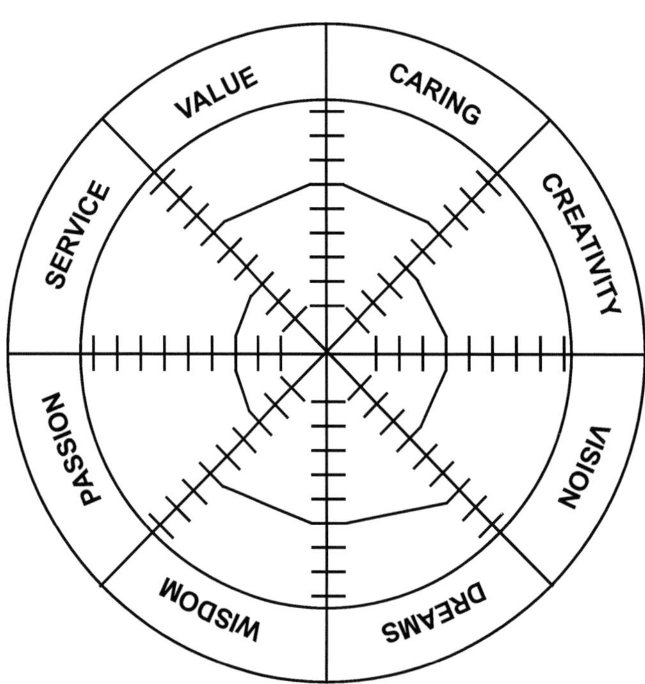

Life Unit
You as an individual

Note: What you are doing here is transferring your selected Life Units to the Wheel of Focus. Here, as explained in the *Life's Journey* book, you are simply bringing together those Life Units you have identified as significant.

3. **Graph out your Desired Future for selected Life Units on the Wheel of Focus.** By connecting (graphing out) your identified Desired Future for each Life Unit, you have brought into full view your chosen future. This represents where you want to be. This is the destination you have chosen for your own life.

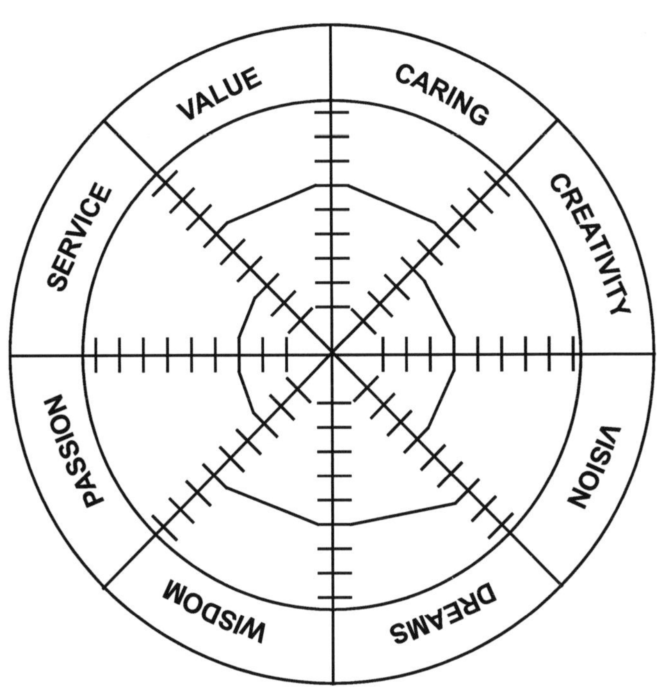

Life Unit
You as an individual

Note: Again, you are transferring your selected Life Units to the Wheel of Focus.

4. **Identify the gaps that exist (if any) between where you are currently at and your determined future.** This awareness gives you the ability to gauge the distance required for your journey of self-growth and achievement. It is the map and realization that will assist you in determining what actions, tools, knowledge, and skills will be required to successfully make the trip.

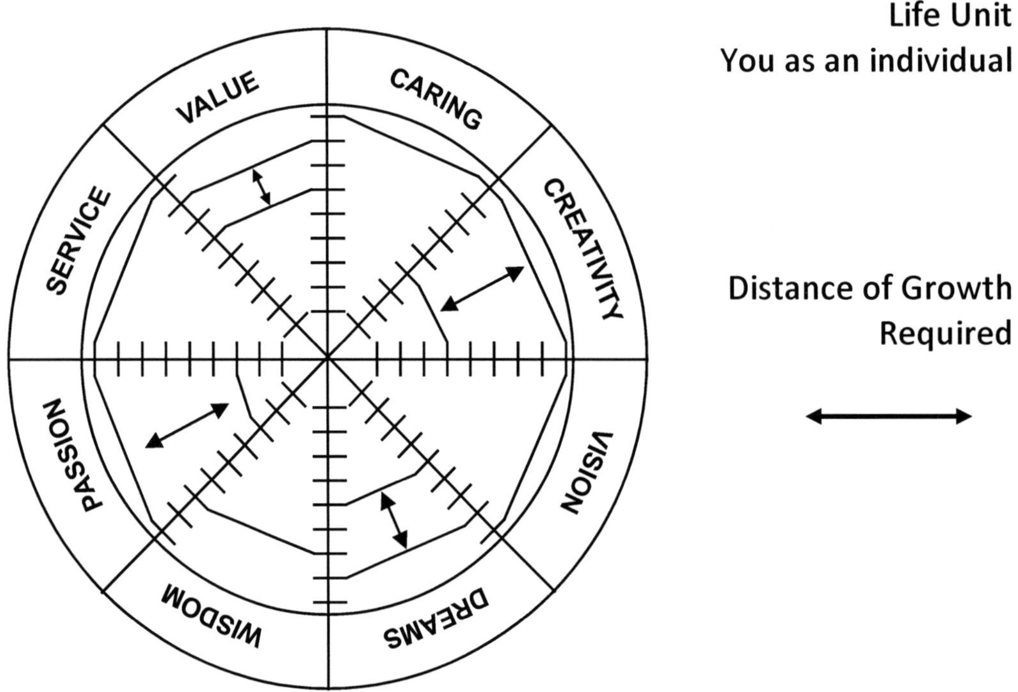

Life Unit
You as an individual

Distance of Growth
Required

Note: This provides you with a wonderful visualization and awareness of the journey before you. Your effectiveness to make decisions producing specific actions is based on this awareness. It is a simple yet powerful demonstration of that necessary growth (gap) required to achieve your destination.

5. **Identify *specific actions* to build your performance bridge from where you are currently at to your own future (where you want to be).** This is one of the most difficult parts of the process. What exactly will it take to move you from where you are to where you need to be? This is why your sincere and intense concentration on each of the Life Unit chapters is so important. Your focus on each of these leads to a heightened awareness of what specific actions, behavior, knowledge, and skills will be necessary for you to obtain or take. You will find the last page of each Life Unit particularly helpful in this part of the process. Please review and record your final specific decisions in your *Life's Journey Personal Journal.*

6. Transfer each Wheel of Focus to your Life Pattern. Please note: You are not limited to only one Life Focus Area. Should you exceed the recommended number of Life Units (eight) for a Life Focus Area, simply create another again with a maximum of eight Life Units to be included. You may also find that you have other Life Focus Areas you wish to add. Simply follow the identified process for each area of concentration. However, we do recommend that you do not exceed four Life Focus Areas. Again, this is for the purpose of effective concentration. Each Life Focus Area will be displayed on a Wheel of Focus that makes up your Life Pattern.

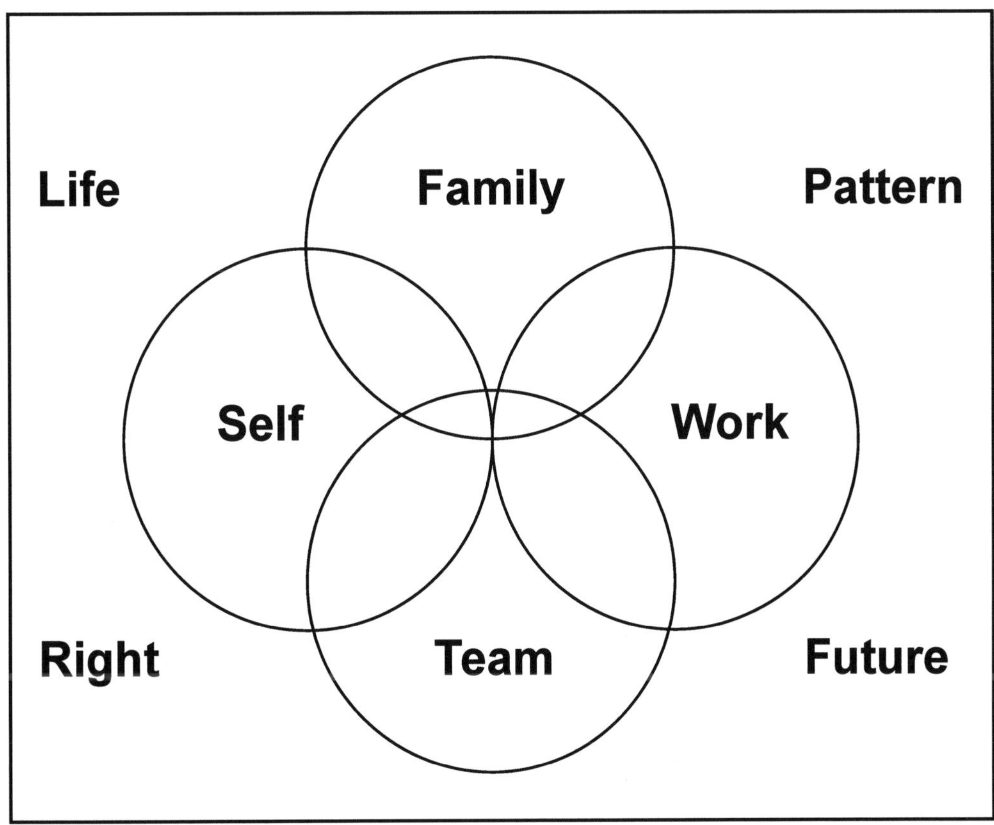

Let's say that you have selected the following Life Focus Areas: Self, Family, Work, and Team. Together they form an interdependent relationship to form your Life Pattern. This interconnection of Life Focus Areas presents an even more complete picture of you and your right future.

7. **Give yourself permission to take action and create your own future.**
    Only you can do this! You have all the tools before you. You personally
    selected Life Focus Areas because you believe they are critical to your very
    existence. You further identified the primary components (Life Units) of
    each Life Focus Area. You then charted and graphed out your Place to Stand
    (where you are currently at) and your desired future (where you want to
    be). You then identified specific actions, which, if taken, will achieve for you
    your goals and pathways to success. You have attained critical unification
    and all is at a readiness level to act. You've come so far at this point in time.
    However, all is for naught if you do not give yourself permission to proceed.
    Build it! Achieve it! Become it! You have earned the right to bring to yourself
    that which only you can bring—your own future!

8. **Use your *Life's Journey Personal Journal* to track and document your
    progress.** Your own personal journal is included to document your deci-
    sions, your actions, your personal insights, and whatever else you choose to
    include that complements and supports your journey. Here you may record
    your daily/weekly/monthly/yearly progress. The journal pages are for the
    documentation of your own progress, questions, concerns, and feelings
    encountered as you move toward your Right Future.

Awareness +
Permission to Act =
Power Over Your Own Future

The Wheel of Focus

The Wheel of Focus represents an overview and guide of each selected Life Unit. Select the appropriate Life Units that relate to you in your particular situation and area you are choosing to concentrate on at this moment in time. Your Life Area Focus (which is visually displayed by the wheel) is critical to your journey of discovery.

Your focus may be on areas that may include, but are not limited to, any of the following:

- self
- family
- team
- company
- organization
- church
- group
- corporation
- partner (friend, spouse, significant other)
- business
- relationship
- other

Once you have decided upon your Life Area Focus, review and select for the wheel those Life Units that you feel relate significantly to your focus or area of concentration. You may choose any or all areas to concentrate on (some samples are listed for your review). Identify your current position and your desired future destination. Decide on specific actions, behaviors, knowledge, skills, and other essential factors necessary to construct the bridge from where you are to where you want to be. You now have your plan of action and have attained **critical unification.** This coming together and achievement of awareness is *your signal to act.* Give yourself permission to begin your journey while charting your progress along the way. Celebrate your achievements as you move toward your own future.

Make your choices sincerely and with great care, for they truly will impact your own future. Give yourself permission to choose, for failure to choose is a choice in and of itself and it can become the choice you find yourself having to live with. Can anyone afford not to make these choices, the choices of our own life, of our own future?

Awareness + Permission to Act = Power Over Your Own Future

The sum total of your critical unifying components = YOU

What Life Units are required for your success with the Life Focus Area you have selected (self, team, family, company, etc.)? What other units are critical to the survival of your focus area?

Below are samples of Life Units that may be selected for various Life Focus Areas. Please do not limit yourself to our suggestions. These are areas we have found to be of significant concern by individuals, organizations, and companies we have had the pleasure to work with.

Outside Sales Force of a company:

The Right Partnership	The Right Order
The Right Value	The Right Service
The Right Fit	The Right Change
The Right Responsiveness	The Right Reaction

Leadership of an organization:

The Right Change	The Right Passion
The Right Creativity	The Right Change
The Right Vision	The Right Dreams
The Right Wisdom	The Right Permission

You as an individual:

<table>
<tr><td>The Right Value</td><td>The Right Dreams</td></tr>
<tr><td>The Right Caring</td><td>The Right Wisdom</td></tr>
<tr><td>The Right Vision</td><td>The Right Passion</td></tr>
<tr><td>The Right Choice</td><td>The Right Success</td></tr>
</table>

Family:

<table>
<tr><td>The Right Value</td><td>The Right Dreams</td></tr>
<tr><td>The Right Opportunity</td><td>The Right Passion</td></tr>
<tr><td>The Right Vision</td><td>The Right Love</td></tr>
<tr><td>The Right Caring</td><td>The Right Wisdom</td></tr>
</table>

Church or religious organization:

<table>
<tr><td>The Right Fit</td><td>The Right Service</td></tr>
<tr><td>The Right Caring</td><td>The Right Vision</td></tr>
<tr><td>The Right Passion</td><td>The Right Value</td></tr>
<tr><td>The Right Love</td><td>The Right Giving</td></tr>
</table>

Volunteer organization:

<table>
<tr><td>The Right Caring</td><td>The Right Service</td></tr>
<tr><td>The Right Love</td><td>The Right Responsiveness</td></tr>
<tr><td>The Right Giving</td><td>The Right Value</td></tr>
<tr><td>The Right Permission</td><td>The Right Opportunity</td></tr>
</table>

Group or team:

<table>
<tr><td>The Right Wisdom</td><td>The Right Partnership</td></tr>
<tr><td>The Right Creativity</td><td>The Right "I"</td></tr>
<tr><td>The Right "We"</td><td>The Right Passion</td></tr>
<tr><td>The Right Caring</td><td>The Right Success</td></tr>
</table>

Note: The "Focus on Self" section should be completed for all Life Focus Areas. It is absolutely critical to analyze, review, and raise your own awareness of your journey up to this moment in your life. Your sincerity and time spent in answering the thoughtful insights contained in this section, as specifically as you can, will have an enormous effect on decisions made to create your own future.

We all have choices before us:
Will you worry and hope, or create and build?

Please choose to create.

Please choose to build.

Critical Unification is that point where all is at a readiness level to take action. It is the bringing together of all identified Life Units in your Life Focus Area that together equal your Right Future. When you become a master of yourself, you recognize when that moment is attained and allow yourself to respond by taking action and doing that which is right, necessary, and proper to ensure your own growth.

The Wheel of Focus will present you with a *visual awareness* of your strengths, your opportunities for improvement and growth, your pros and cons or pluses and minuses. You can see the total package of what makes you and enables you to stand firm in your own realization of self. You then (and only you) have the authority to permit yourself to build from that base and construct through specific actions that future you have chose to possess.

The more you fortify your wheel by raising your awareness of each critical Life Unit you have identified, the stronger you become as a total person. As your wheel becomes complete and you achieve Critical Unification, you are building the necessary mechanisms to withstand attacks upon your own well-being.

Awareness + Permission to Act = Power Over Your Own Future

Perhaps you have experienced the following scenario. The weather is very foul. The snow accumulation has practically shut down the city with no end to the storm in sight. You're out at the main airport bewildered as to how to get from where you are currently at to where you want and need to be in order to accomplish your goals. People are counting on you to be there. Your arrival at your destination is expected and your inability to arrive will be a disappointment to a number of individuals. Unfortunately you are at the mercy of a number of variables of which you have no control. Some of these include the weather, the airport conditions and the personnel at the airport who make significant deci-sions, which will certainly impact your situation. You have become a victim of these circumstances, which will either allow you to journey to your final destination or remain where you are.

There are some similarities between this scenario and the Wheel of Focus and some very significant differences. Your Right Future as the traveler is to accomplish your goal by arriving at your chosen destination on time to meet with those who are counting on you to be there. You have thought out and planned your "units" or right components, that you believed would equal that Right Future. Some of these include travel arrangements, tickets, being packed and ready to go, arrival at the airport in a timely manner, proper check-in at the appropriate airline, bags checked, presenting all of the appropriate identifications, going through security, walking to the proper gate, and being present and accounted for (ready to board). Again, these are the components that you believe equal the Right Future.

The Wheel of Focus is intended to raise your level of awareness and the control you have over your own future as you identify specific actions to take that will create that future. The airport scenario contains many components outside the realm of the wheel of focus—items, which the traveler has no control over and is powerless to do anything about. Decisions made by airport officials to keep open or shut down the airport, decisions by the airline itself to postpone or cancel the flight, and the overall weather conditions are out of the traveler's control.

The Wheel of Focus concentrates on your power over your own future and your ability through your own actions to create that future. **It is a purposeful journey of change.** You place the responsibility upon yourself to be accountable for yourself in accomplishing your own movement from where you are to where you need to be. You're responsible; you're in control of your own destiny and not a victim at the mercy of others.

Of course, there may be (and we'd be foolish not to expect them) unforeseen setbacks. However, our movement toward our future is set and our focus is on what we can do in its achievement and not on external components working to prevent that future from being realized. Our concentration is on those items *you can control and/or have a significant impact upon* and, in turn, how they impact you.

Note: What follows is a sample Wheel of Focus. Eight identified Life Units were chosen to complete the wheel. Remember that you may wish to fill out more than one Wheel of Focus depending on the intricacies of your life. That would then form a Life Pattern. Following the sample are a number of blank Wheels of Focus for your own use.

The Wheel of Focus
Sample

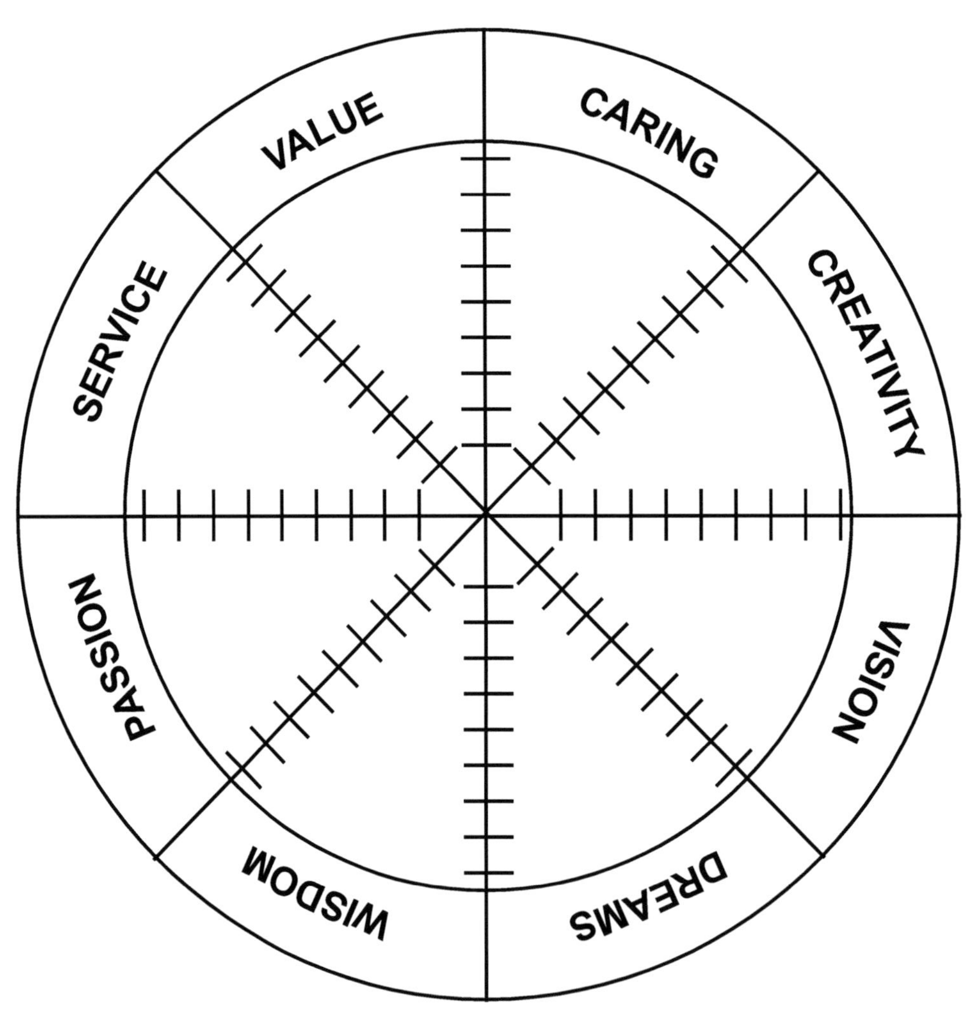

The Wheel of Focus

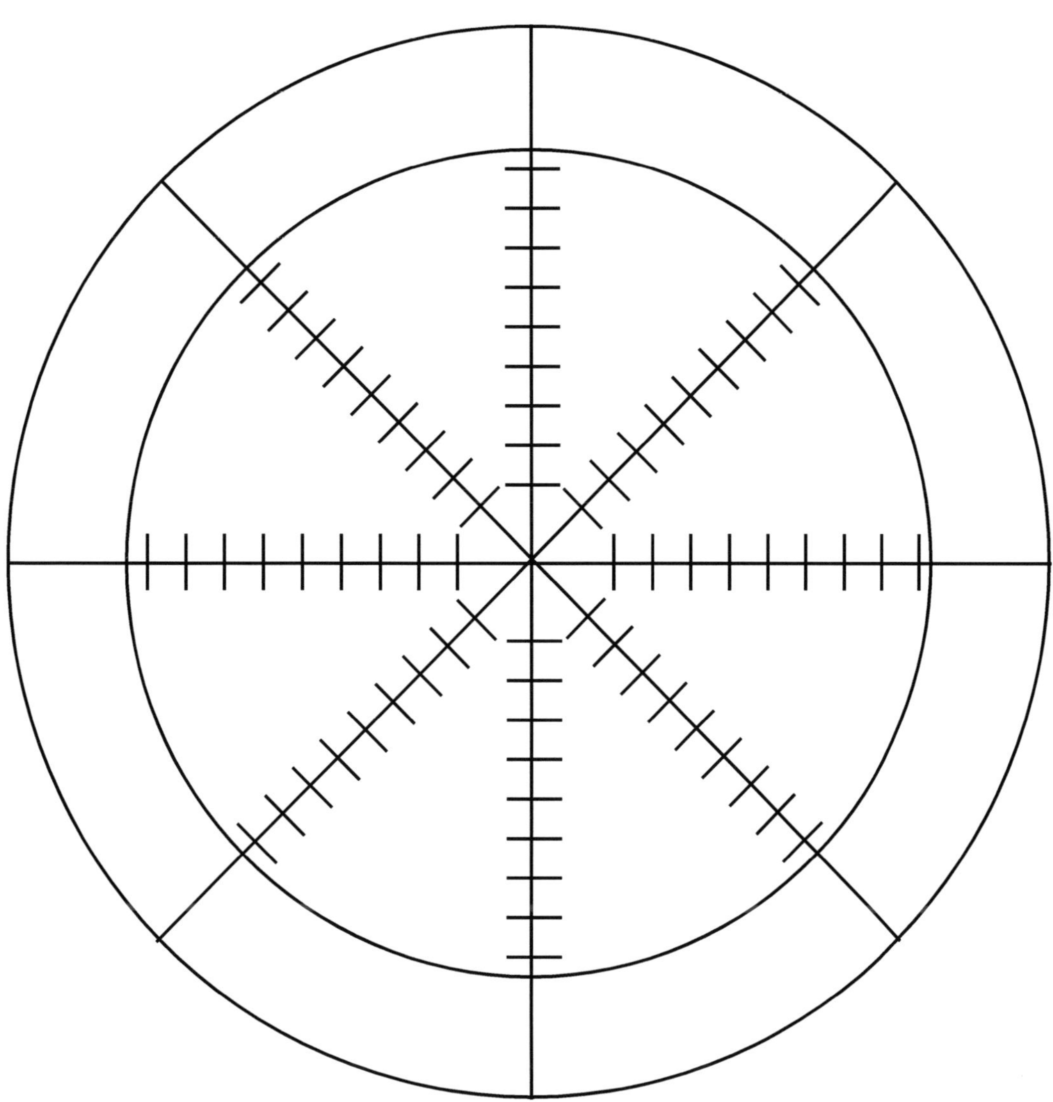

The Wheel of Focus

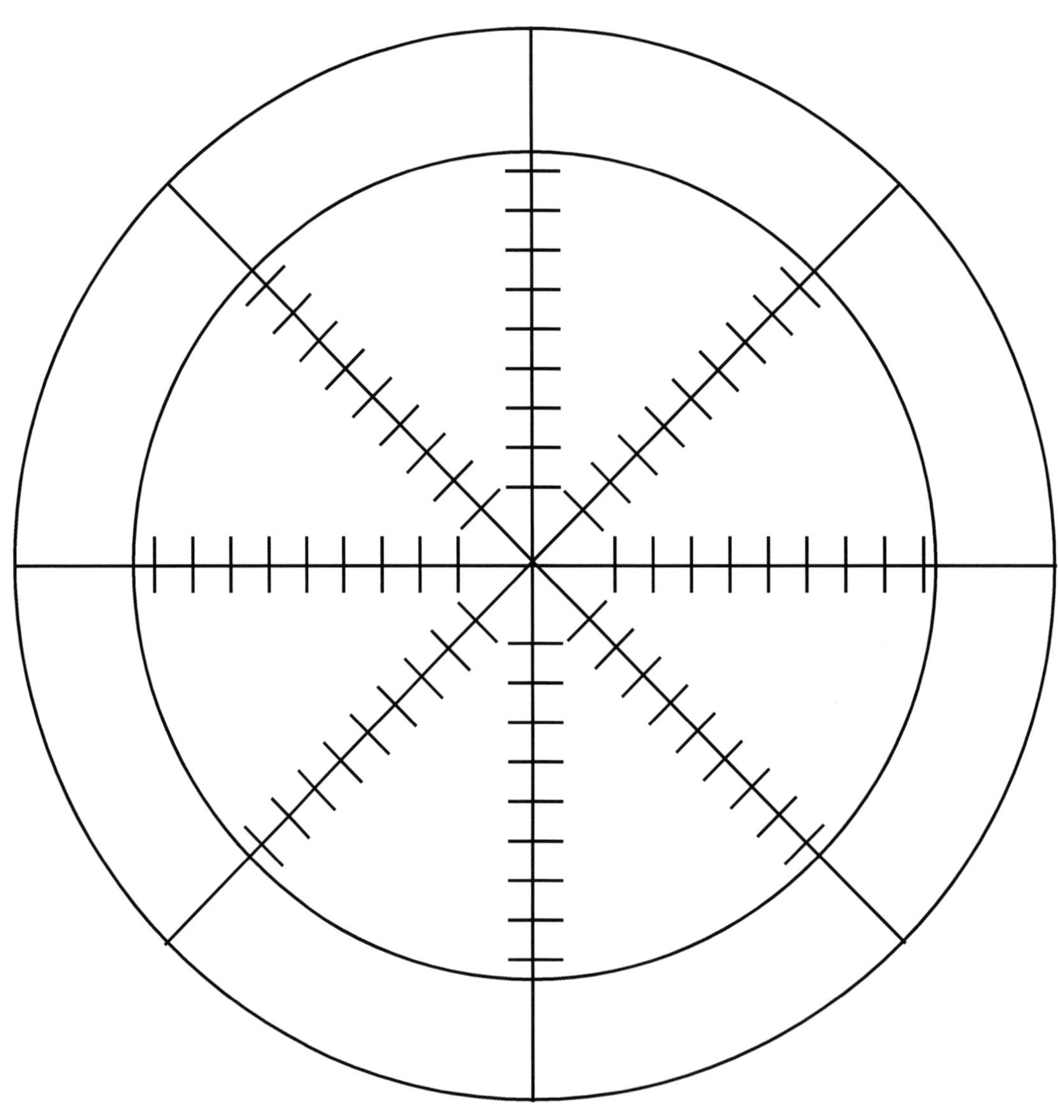

The Wheel of Focus

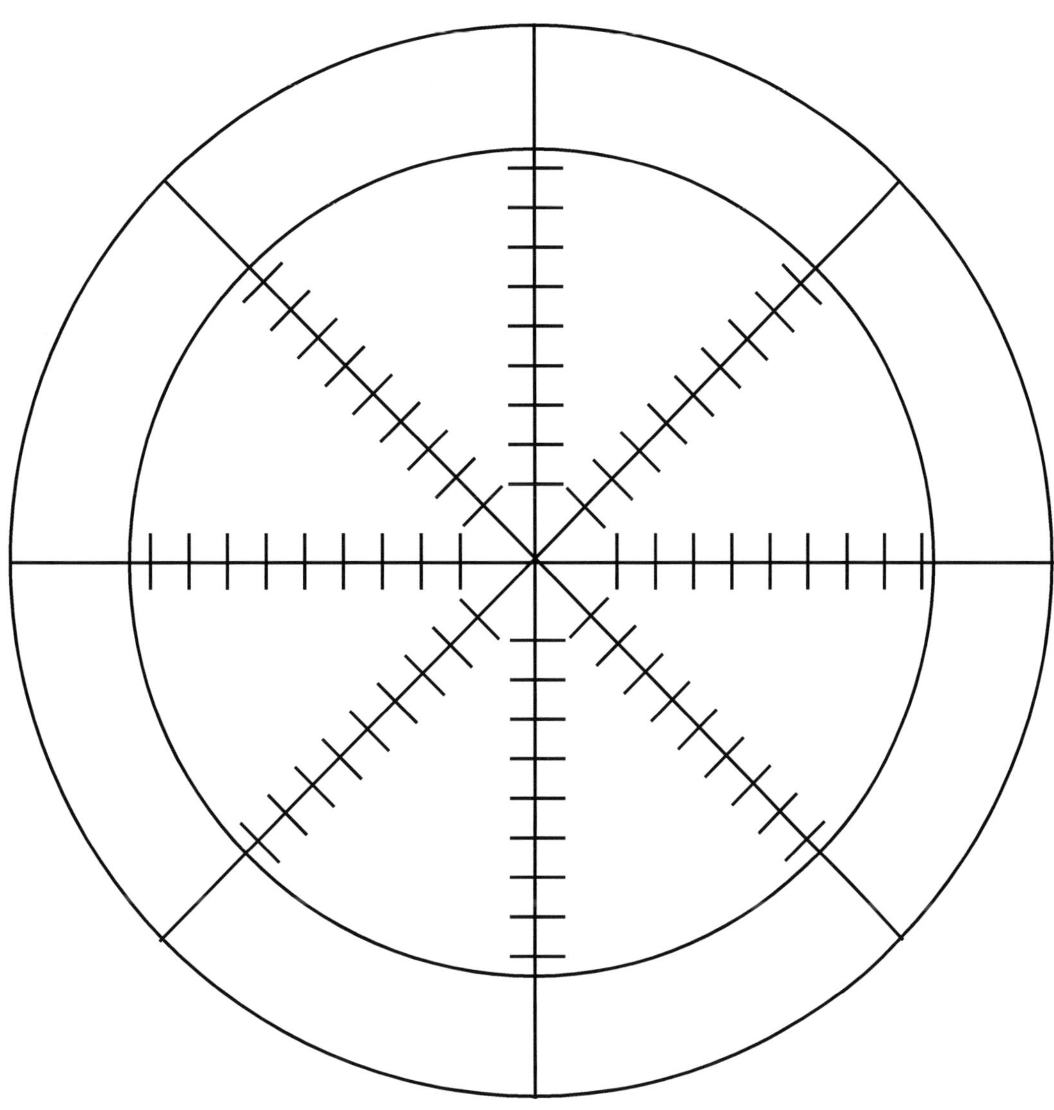

The Wheel of Focus

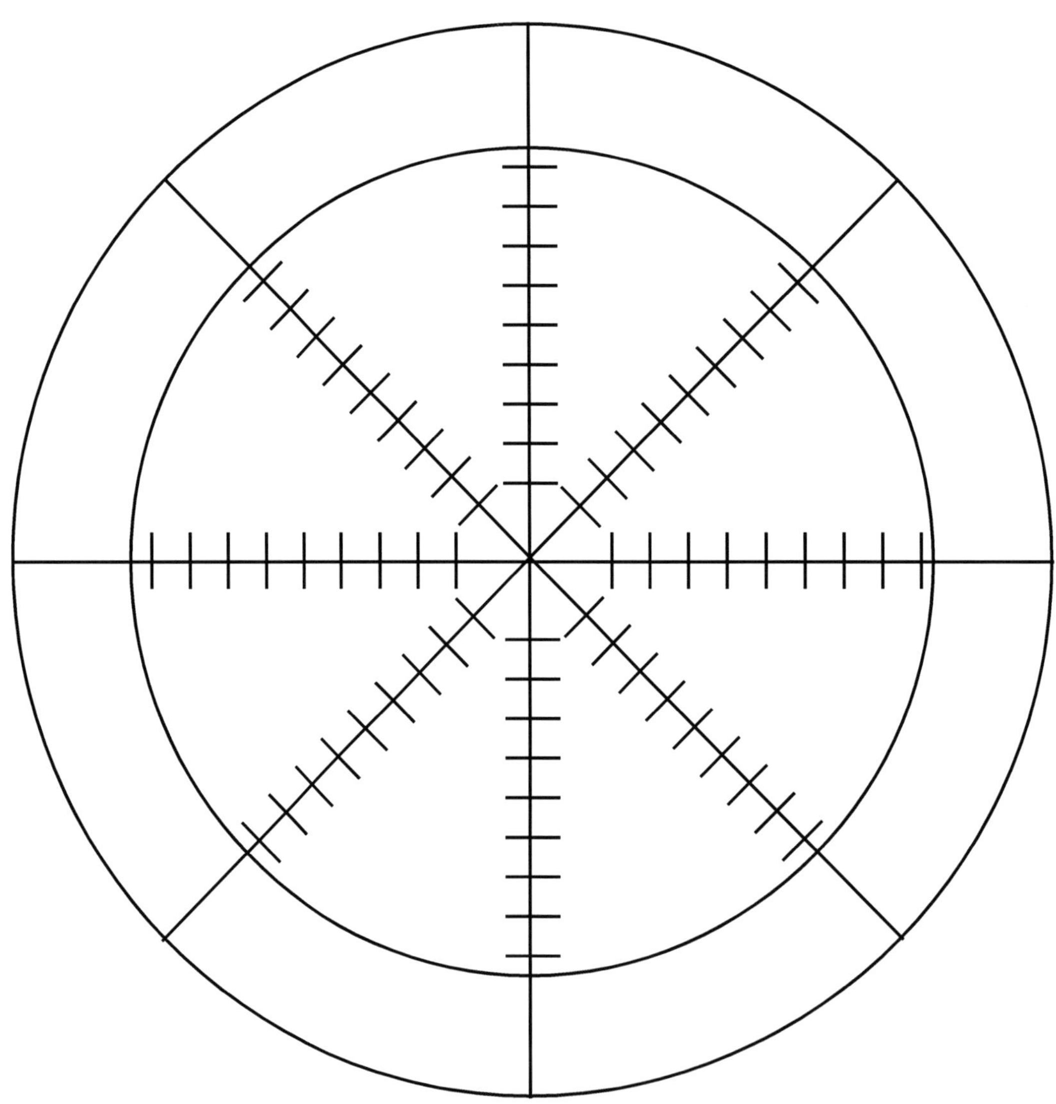

The Wheel of Focus

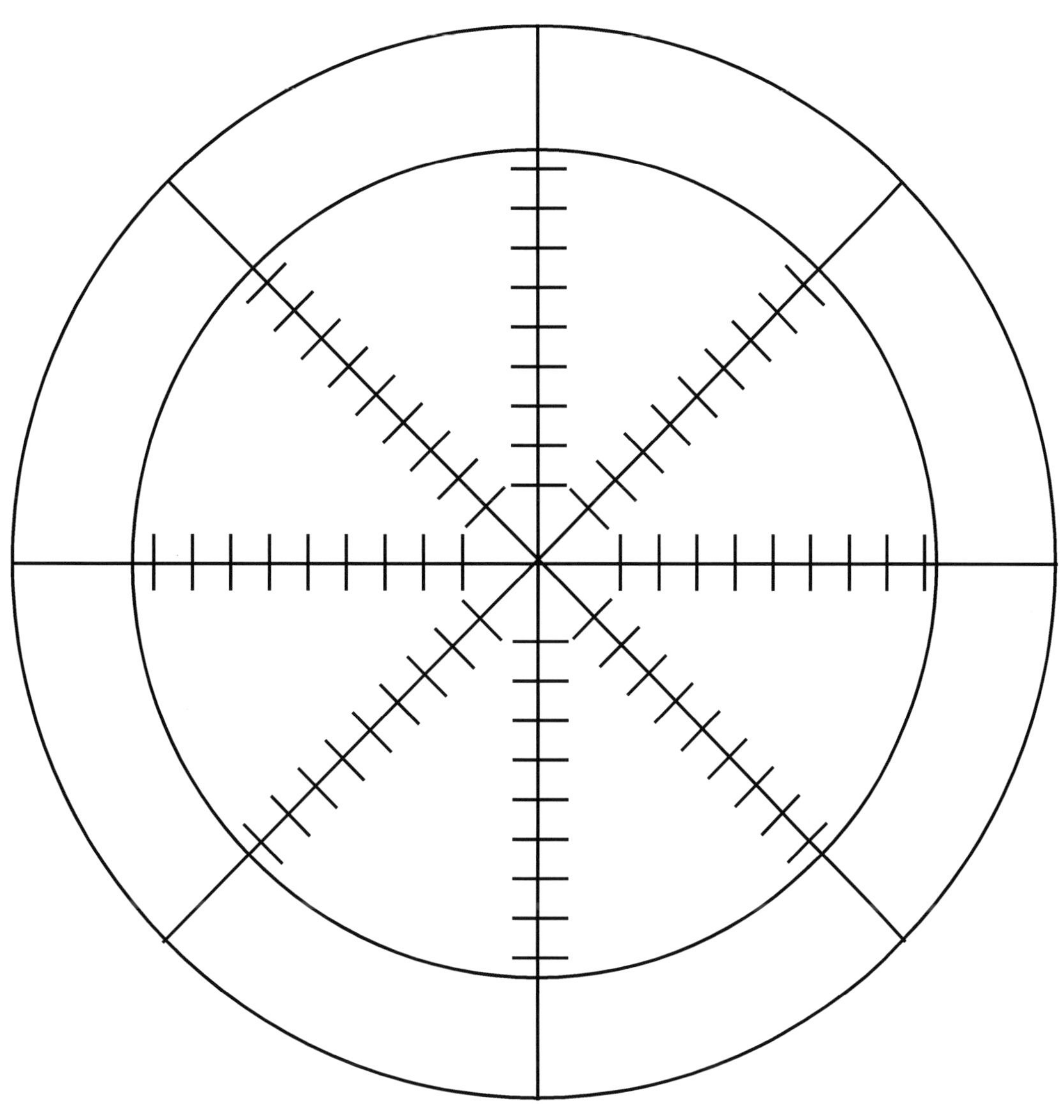

The Wheel of Focus

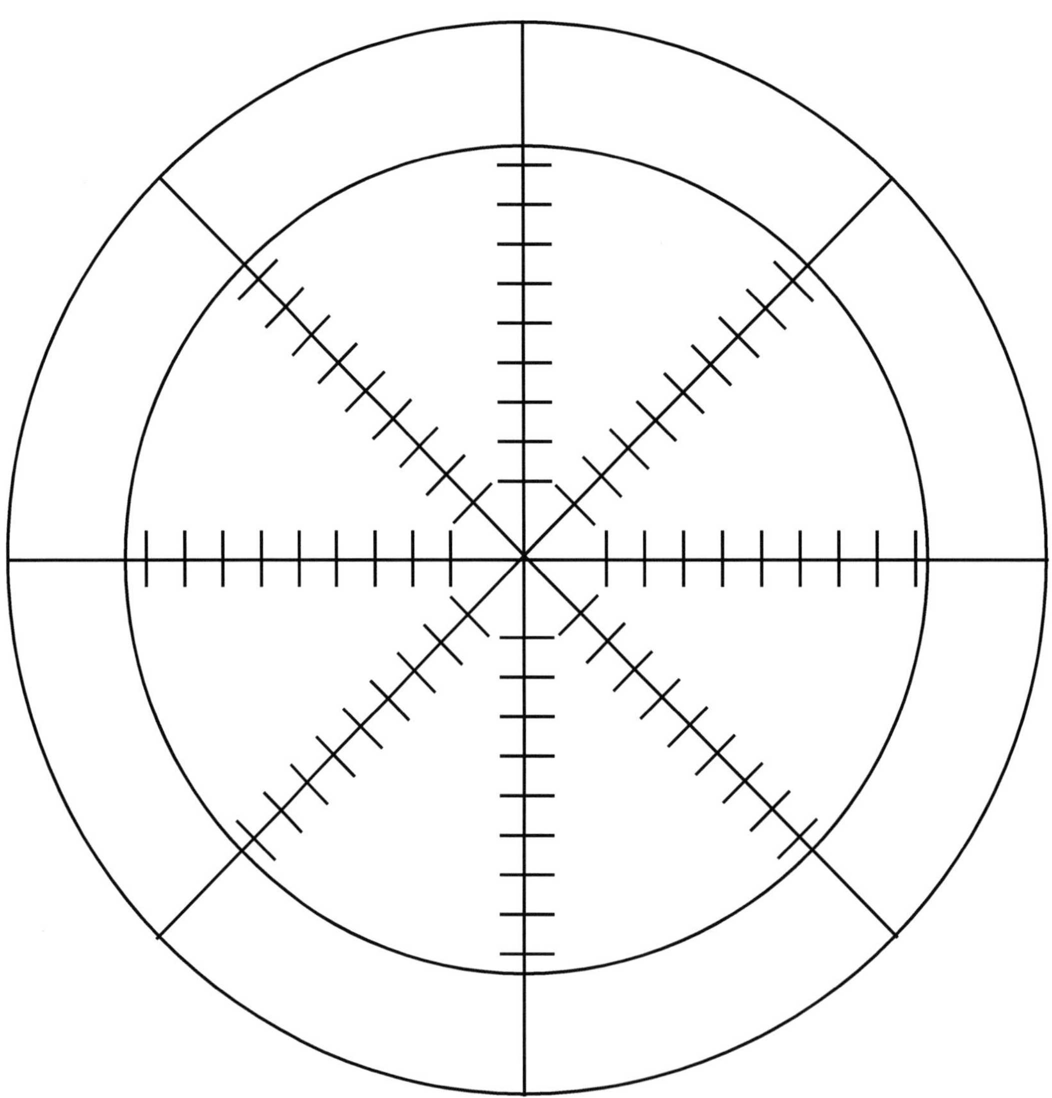

The Wheel of Focus

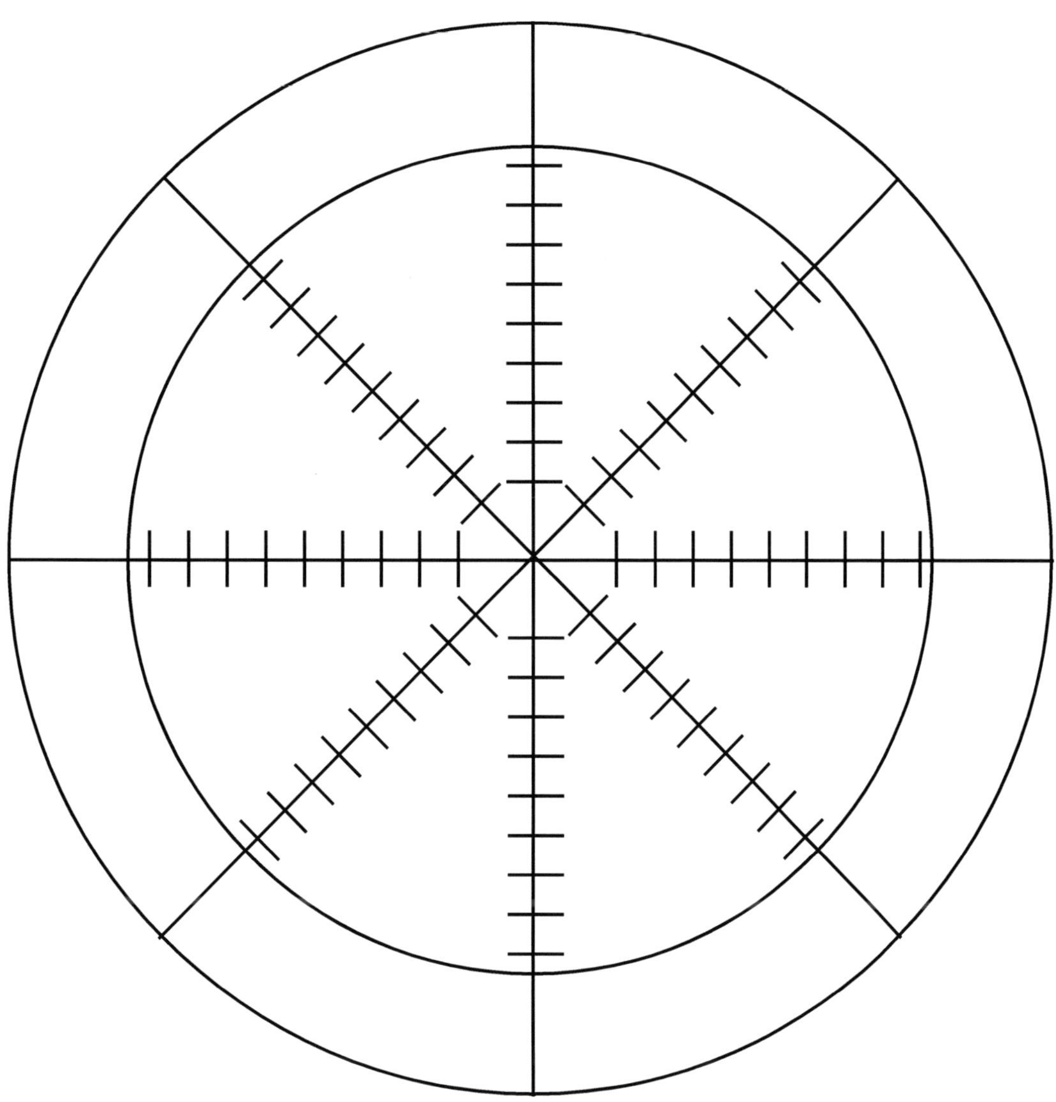

> # Your future is not
> # a matter of chance,
> # but a matter of choice!

Journal Entry

Here is what I did today to move myself toward my own future:

Date: _____________________

"Nothing can bring you peace but yourself."

– Ralph Waldo Emerson

Journal Entry

Here is what I did today to move myself toward my own future:

Date: ___________________

> *"Behold the turtle. He only makes progress when he sticks his neck out."*
>
> — James Bryant Conant

Journal Entry

Here is what I did today to move myself toward my own future:

Date: _______________________

> "If we have not peace within ourselves, it is in vain to seek it from outward sources."
>
> — Francois de La Rochefoncauld

Journal Entry

Here is what I did today to move myself toward my own future:

Date: _______________________

Journal Entry

Here is what I did today to move myself toward my own future:

Date: ______________________

> *"To understand is to forgive, even yourself."*
> — Alexander Chase

Journal Entry

Here is what I did today to move myself toward my own future:

Date: _______________________

> *"Does't thou love life? Then do not squander time, for that is the stuff life is made of."*
>
> — Benjamin Franklin

Journal Entry

Here is what I did today to move myself toward my own future:

Date: ___________________________

> *"How many things there are which I do not want."*
>
> — Socrates

Journal Entry

Here is what I did today to move myself toward my own future:

Date: ___________________________

"Ignorance is the curse of God. Knowledge
the wing wherewith we fly to heaven."

– William Shakespeare, *Henry VI.*

Journal Entry

Here is what I did today to move myself toward my own future:

Date: _______________________

> *"Only the person who has faith in himself is able to be faithful to others."*
>
> – Erich Fromm

Journal Entry

Here is what I did today to move myself toward my own future:

Date: ___________________________

> *"Don't go around saying the world owes you a living; the world owes you nothing; it was here first."*
>
> — Alexander Chase

Journal Entry

Here is what I did today to move myself toward my own future:

Date: _______________________

> *"Knowing others is wisdom; knowing yourself is enlightenment."*
>
> — Lao-tzu

Journal Entry

Here is what I did today to move myself toward my own future:

Date: _______________________

> *"It is not the strongest of the species that survive, nor the most intelligent, but the one most responsive to change."*
>
> — Charles Darwin

Journal Entry

Here is what I did today to move myself toward my own future:

Date: ___________________________

> *"No man remains quite what he was when he recognizes himself.""*
>
> — Thomas Mann

Journal Entry

Here is what I did today to move myself toward my own future:

Date: ___________________________

> *"You miss 100% of the shots you never take."*
>
> – Wayne Gretsky

Journal Entry

Here is what I did today to move myself toward my own future:

Date: _______________________

> *"Growth begins when we start to accept our own weakness."*
>
> — Jean Vamier

Journal Entry

Here is what I did today to move myself toward my own future:

Date: ________________________

> "Your reason and your passion are the rudder and the sails of your seafaring soul. If either your sails or your rudder be broken, you can but toss and drift, or else be held at a standstill in mid-seas."
>
> — Kahlil Gibran, *The Prophet*

Journal Entry

Here is what I did today to move myself toward my own future:

Date: ___________________________

> "Self-confidence is the first requisite to great undertakings."
>
> — Samuel Johnson

Journal Entry

Here is what I did today to move myself toward my own future:

Date: _____________________

> *"Nothing great was ever achieved without enthusiasm."*
>
> — Ralph Waldo Emerson

Journal Entry

Here is what I did today to move myself toward my own future:

Date: _______________________

Journal Entry

Here is what I did today to move myself toward my own future:

Date: _______________________

> *"If man wants his dreams to come true, he must wake up."*
>
> — Anonymous

Journal Entry

Here is what I did today to move myself toward my own future:

Date: ______________________

> *"If your ship doesn't come in, swim out to it."*
>
> — Jonathan Winters

Journal Entry

Here is what I did today to move myself toward my own future:

Date: _______________________

> *"Take your life in your own hands, and what happens? A terrible thing; no one to blame."*
>
> — Erica Jong

Journal Entry

Here is what I did today to move myself toward my own future:

Date: ________________________

> *"Of all sad words of tongue or pen, the saddest are these: It might have been."*
>
> — John Greenleaf Whittier

Journal Entry

Here is what I did today to move myself toward my own future:

Date: _______________________

> *"Yesterday is a cancelled check. Tomorrow is a promissory note. Today is cash in hand. Spend it!"*
>
> — John W. Newbern

Journal Entry

Here is what I did today to move myself toward my own future:

Date: _______________________

> *"I fear there will be no future for those who do not change."*
>
> — Louis L'Amour

Journal Entry

Here is what I did today to move myself toward my own future:

Date: _______________________

"No one can defeat us unless we first defeat ourselves."

— Dwight D. Eisenhower

Journal Entry

Here is what I did today to move myself toward my own future:

Date: _______________________

> *"When we can't dream any longer, we die."*
> — Emma Goldman

Journal Entry

Here is what I did today to move myself toward my own future:

Date: _______________________

> *"A man's fortune must first be changed from within."*
>
> — Chinese proverb

Journal Entry

Here is what I did today to move myself toward my own future:

Date: _______________________

> *"This above all: to thine own self be true."*
> — William Shakespeare

Journal Entry

Here is what I did today to move myself toward my own future:

Date: _______________________

> *"Resolve to be thyself... he who finds himself loses his misery!"*
>
> — Matthew Arnold

Journal Entry

Here is what I did today to move myself toward my own future:

Date: ______________________

"The only thing we have to fear is fear itself… nameless, unreasoning, unjustified terror which paralyzes needed efforts to convert retreat into advance."

— Franklin Delano Roosevelt

Journal Entry

Here is what I did today to move myself toward my own future:

Date: ___________________________

> *"Your daily life is your temple and your religion.*
> *Whenever you enter into it take with you your all."*
>
> – Kahlil Gibran, *The Prophet*

Journal Entry

Here is what I did today to move myself toward my own future:

Date: _______________________

____
____
____
____
____
____
____
____
____
____
____
____
____
____
____
____
____
____

> *"True success is overcoming the fear of being successful."*
>
> – Paul Sweeney

Journal Entry

Here is what I did today to move myself toward my own future:

Date: _______________________

> *"Go forth to meet the shadowy future without fear and with a manly heart."*
>
> — Henry Wadsworth Longfellow

Journal Entry

Here is what I did today to move myself toward my own future:

Date: ____________________

> *"If you want to conquer fear, don't sit at home
> and think about it. Go out and get busy."*
>
> — Dale Carnegie

Journal Entry

Here is what I did today to move myself toward my own future:

Date: _______________________

> *"If you are doing your best, you will not have time to worry about failure."*
>
> — Robert Hillyer

Journal Entry

Here is what I did today to move myself toward my own future:

Date: ___________________

> "Freedom is nothing else but a chance to be better, whereas enslavement is a certainty of the worst."
>
> — Albert Camus

Journal Entry

Here is what I did today to move myself toward my own future:

Date: ___________________

____

____

____

____

____

____

____

____

____

____

____

____

____

____

____

____

____

____

____

"Doubt whom you will, but never yourself."
— Christian Bovee

Journal Entry

Here is what I did today to move myself toward my own future:

Date: ___________________________

> *"Only those who dare to fail greatly can ever achieve greatly."*
>
> — Robert F. Kennedy

Journal Entry

Here is what I did today to move myself toward my own future:

Date: _______________________

____

____

____

____

____

____

____

____

____

____

____

____

____

____

____

____

____

____

> *"It is impossible to win the great prizes of life without running risks."*
>
> — **Theodore Roosevelt**

Journal Entry

Here is what I did today to move myself toward my own future:

Date: _______________________

> *"Have the courage to live. Anyone can die."*
>
> — Robert Cody

Journal Entry

Here is what I did today to move myself toward my own future:

Date: _______________________

> *"It is our duty as men and women to proceed as though limits to our abilities do not exist."*
>
> – Pierre Teilhard de Chardin

Journal Entry

Here is what I did today to move myself toward my own future:

Date: _______________________

____

____

____

____

____

____

____

____

____

____

____

____

____

____

____

____

____

____

> *"A journey of a thousand miles must begin with a single step."*
>
> — Chinese proverb

Journal Entry

Here is what I did today to move myself toward my own future:

Date: _______________________

> *"Knowing is not enough, we must apply.*
> *Willing is not enough, we must do."*
>
> – Johann von Goethe

Journal Entry

Here is what I did today to move myself toward my own future:

Date: _______________________

Journal Entry

Here is what I did today to move myself toward my own future:

Date: ___________________

> *"Success follows doing what you want to do.*
> *There is no other way to be successful."*
>
> – Malcolm Forbes

Journal Entry

Here is what I did today to move myself toward my own future:

Date: ___________________________

> *"I am prepared to meet my Maker. Whether my Maker is prepared for the great ordeal of meeting me is another matter."*
>
> — Winston Churchill

Journal Entry

Here is what I did today to move myself toward my own future:

Date: _______________________

> *"Pessimism is only the name that men of weak nerves give to wisdom."*
>
> — Bernard De Voto

Journal Entry

Here is what I did today to move myself toward my own future:

Date: _______________________

> *"Believe that life is worth living, and your belief will help create the fact."*
>
> — William James

Journal Entry

Here is what I did today to move myself toward my own future:

Date: _______________________

> *"No man, who continues to add something to the material, intellectual and moral well-being of the place in which he lives, is left long without proper reward."*
>
> — Booker T. Washington

Journal Entry

Here is what I did today to move myself toward my own future:

Date: _______________________

> *"To believe your own thought, to believe that what is true for you in your private heart is true for all men—that is genius."*
>
> — Ralph Waldo Emerson

Journal Entry

Here is what I did today to move myself toward my own future:

Date: _______________________

> *"Resolve to be tender with the young, compassionate with the aged, sympathetic with the striving, and tolerant with the weak and wrong... because sometime in your life you will have been all of these."*
>
> — Anonymous

Journal Entry

Here is what I did today to move myself toward my own future:

Date: _______________________

> *"If we want to change a situation, we first have to change ourselves. And to change ourselves effectively, we first have to change our perceptions."*
>
> — Dr. Stephen Covey

Journal Entry

Here is what I did today to move myself toward my own future:

Date: _______________________

> *"Attitudes are contagious. Is yours worth catching?"*
>
> — Anonymous

Journal Entry

Here is what I did today to move myself toward my own future:

Date: ______________________

> *"The credit belongs to those people who are actually in the arena… who know the great enthusiasms, the great devotions to a worthy cause; who at best, know the triumph of high achievement; and who, at worst, fail while daring greatly… so that their place shall never be with those cold and timid souls who know neither victory nor defeat."*
>
> — Theodore Roosevelt

Journal Entry

Here is what I did today to move myself toward my own future:

Date: ______________________

> *"If you chase two rabbits, both will escape."*
>
> — Ancient proverb

Journal Entry

Here is what I did today to move myself toward my own future:

Date: _______________________

> *"Goals are the bridges that span our dreams."*
>
> — Anonymous

Journal Entry

Here is what I did today to move myself toward my own future:

Date: _______________________

> *"We're all only fragile thread, but what a tapestry we make."*
>
> — Jerry Ellis

Journal Entry

Here is what I did today to move myself toward my own future:

Date: _______________________

> *"The most important lesson you can learn
> from winning is that you can."*
>
> — Dave Weinbaum

Journal Entry

Here is what I did today to move myself toward my own future:

Date: _______________________

(journal writing lines)

> *"At some time in your life, you probably had someone believe in you when you didn't believe in yourself. They scripted you. Did that make a difference in your life? What if you were a positive scripter, an affirmer, of other people?"*
>
> — Dr. Stephen Covey

Journal Entry

Here is what I did today to move myself toward my own future:

Date: _______________________

> *"I'm just a slinky on the stairway of life."*
>
> — **Bumper sticker**

Journal Entry

Here is what I did today to move myself toward my own future:

Date: _______________________

> *"The improvement of our way of life is more important than the spreading of it. If we make it satisfactory enough, it will spread automatically. If we do not, no strength of arms can permanently oppose it."*
>
> – Charles A. Lindbergh

Journal Entry

Here is what I did today to move myself toward my own future:

Date: _________________________

> *"The block of granite which was an obstacle in the pathway of the weak becomes a stepping stone in the pathway of the strong."*
>
> — Thomas Carlyle

Journal Entry

Here is what I did today to move myself toward my own future:

Date: ________________________

> *"If you accept the expectation of others, especially negative ones, then you never will change the outcome."*
>
> — Michael Jordan

Journal Entry

Here is what I did today to move myself toward my own future:

Date: _______________________

> *"The soul is dyed the color of its thoughts. Think only on those things that are in line with your principles and can bear the full light of day. The content of your character is your choice. Day by day, what you choose, what you think, and what you do is who you become. Your integrity is your destiny… It is the light that guides your way."*
>
> **– Heraclitus: Greek Poet/Philosopher**

Journal Entry

Here is what I did today to move myself toward my own future:

Date: ______________________

"You can't have the fruits without the roots. It's the principle of sequencing: Private victory precedes public victory. Self-mastery and self-discipline are the foundation of good relationships with others."

— Dr. Stephen Covey

Journal Entry

Here is what I did today to move myself toward my own future:

Date: _______________________

> *"The sea is dangerous and its storms terrible, but these obstacles have never been sufficient reason to remain ashore. Unlike the mediocre, intrepid spirits seek victory over those things that seem impossible. It is with an iron will that they embark on the most daring of all endeavors—to meet the shadowy future without fear and conquer the unknown."*
>
> — Ferdinand Magellan

Journal Entry

Here is what I did today to move myself toward my own future:

Date: _______________________

> *"You cannot run away from weakness; you must some time fight it out or perish; and if that be so, why not now, and where you stand?"*
>
> — Robert Louis Stevenson

We would love to hear from you. We welcome your comments, insights, questions, and concerns. You may contact us at info@thelearningservice.com, 2800 Market Avenue North, Canton, OH 44714, or visit our Web site at www.thelearningservice.com.

We wish you well on your Life's Journey!

All our best,

Darryl S. Doane   Rose D. Sloat   David S. Doane

About the Authors

Darryl S. Doane

2800 Market Avenue North, Suite 21
Canton, Ohio 44714
Office: 330-456-2422
info@thelearningservice.com

Darryl Doane has served as a teacher, speaker, facilitator, and professional consultant for over 25 years. He has presented outstanding programs to numerous individuals including adults, college students, youth organizations, churches, civic groups, and businesses.

He facilitates programs that focus on numerous critical issues that include exceptional customer service, sales effectiveness, leadership and managerial skills development, interpersonal relationships, executive coaching, business etiquette, generational differences, and long-term performance improvement. Darryl served as a teacher working with national organizations and was a participant in NASA's Teacher in Space Program. He served as Senior Training Specialist for a billion-dollar corporation for seven years prior to becoming a managing partner and co-creator of The Learning Service, Ltd. He consults and works with clients in a variety of business sectors—agriculture, industrial distribution, health care, finance, higher education, publishing, retail, and manufacturing.

Rose D. Sloat, DTM

2800 Market Avenue North, Suite 21
Canton, Ohio 44714
Office: 330-456-2422

info@thelearningservice.com

Rose Sloat is an outstanding facilitator who has learned, taught, and applied every component within the training arena, from organizing and scheduling training to writing and producing learning events. She facilitates programs that focus on numerous critical issues that include exceptional customer service, sales effectiveness, leadership and managerial skills development, interpersonal relationships, executive coaching, business etiquette, generational differences, and long-term performance improvement. Rose is a managing partner and co-creator of The Learning Service, Ltd. Before forming her company, Rose served as the training coordinator for a billion dollar company for 15 years. Rose brings over 25 years of experience to the training arena. She consults and works with clients in a variety of business sectors—agriculture, industrial distribution, health care, finance, higher education, publishing, retail, and manufacturing.

Rose has been a member of Toastmasters International for the past eight years and has achieved the title of DTM (Distinguished Toastmaster). She has held the positions of Area Governor, President, Vice President of Education, and Secretary. Toastmasters is a fantastic organization and Rose highly recommends it to anyone who wants to improve their communication and leadership skills.

Rose is a member and on the Board of WIN (Women's Initiative), a women's association that supports and recognizes professional and executive women in business. It is a great forum for sharing the wealth of resources and talents of its members.

Darryl's and Rose's published works include:

- The New Sales Game© and The New Sales Game Participant's Book©
- Excuses, Excuses, Excuses for Not Delivering Excellent Customer Service©
- 50 Activities for Achieving Excellent Customer Service©
- Stories They Will Remember©
- The Customer Service Activities Book©
- The Constant Customer—Keep them coming back again and again...©
- Life's Journey—Find Your Place to Stand and Build the Right Future©

Their success results from

- building and maintaining positive relationships;
- building critical bridges of trust and credibility to allow for the sharing of individual and company knowledge and capabilities;
- being a best-selling author with HRD Press and The American Management Association (AMACOM Books);
- offering a wide variety of educational formats and being a proponent of blended learning;
- addressing critical business issues through the implementation of performance-based training and development programs, learning assessments, and e-learning.

David S. Doane

Contributing author to
*Life's Journey—Find Your Place to
Stand and Build the Right Future*

Dr. David Doane has been a practicing psychologist in full-time private practice since 1976, after receiving degrees from Duquesne University (BA), Bowling Green State University (MA), and Kent State University (Ph.D.).

His background includes teaching, supervision, and organizational development. His special interest, however, is in psychotherapy, with a special focus on marriage and family issues. Some writing and presentations round out his professional life. David's programs on marriage and parenting are professional activities that he particularly enjoys and does together with his wife, Barb. A growing interest for David is the harmony of the best of psychology and spirituality, the essence of each being to get one's life together, to heal, and to be whole, which is simultaneously to become holy.

Every individual is part of a bigger system. As Lily Tomlin said, "We're all in this together alone." David's professional bigger systems have provided the nurturing, critiquing, and protection to learn, grow, and go on. His primary and personal bigger system includes Barb and their two adult daughters, Beth and Amy, who certainly help them to appreciate the process and enjoy the present.

David brings a special balance to this particular work, *Life's Journey—Find Your Place to Stand and Build the Right Future*. Near the end of each Life Unit (chapter), there is a section called Musings from the Doctor. In these sections, David shares his expertise and insights with the reader to raise to a higher level of understanding critical issues about themselves regarding their own future.